How To In 2022
By
Amanda Benneyworth

Introduction

1

We've done it, we've reached the 20's, now we just have to find out if they roar like they did 100 years ago. Let's be honest, we've gotten off to a pretty shaky start and if the rest of the decade continues in this manner it's going to be a very bumpy ride.

From social media to lockdowns, from filters to new normals (don't get me started), picking your way through life at the moment is challenging at best and completely depressing at worst. There is one thing that keeps us all going though, humour. You've got to laugh, and believe me, as I go about my daily business there is an awful lot to laugh about.

Join me as I take you on a little journey through life as I see it. In the interests of full disclosure, if you think this book is about you, it is. It's also about me, we are all guilty of a lot of the things that will follow. So, buckle up and prepare to find the funny in the ordinary, because if we can't laugh at ourselves then you've probably bought the wrong book.

How to Navigate Social Media

2

The world has never been more connected. Social media has taken over and we now have the lives of every man and his dog at our fingertips if we so desire. We have intimate access to the daily lives of celebrities as well as the people we went to nursery with 35 years ago and haven't spoken to since. If you can't find an old acquaintance on the socials then the chances are they have sadly not lived to tell the tale or they are living in a cave somewhere at risk of becoming the next star of a reality TV show. #ludditeland

There is so much to say about the online world I could write a whole book, instead I'll give you the edited highlights.

- ❖ If you are having a medical emergency, please let everyone know, write a post about it. Glean opinion from the world's leading armchair doctors and emergency services. Susan from primary school might have seen the rash before and is sure to have advice on the best course of action - cut grass fed into a sock and boiled for four hours cleared hers up in no time.

- ❖ You're having a bad day, mainly because, well, you're having a bad day. Let everyone know BUT do not under any circumstances be specific. In fact, the vaguer the better. When someone notices your bad day and asks what's up, respond with the classic "I'll inbox you hun". Make sure you keep the stealth stalkers among us in the dark, nosiness is most unbecoming.

- ❖ A good deed does not go unpublished. If you find yourself in a situation where you have helped someone, make sure you post it in a way that makes it obvious that you were the anonymous Good Samaritan. Explain that the reason for your post is a well-being check on a nameless person who I'm sure is thrilled to have their traumatic experience, which had been contained to aisle 7 in the supermarket, now made public by the virtue signaller that picked up the eggs and feels worthy of a Pride of Britain award.

- ❖ If you spot someone make a mistake, post it. If you are driving in your car and someone turns left and doesn't use their indicator, it's important that you let your followers know. If you are posting in a community group, always start the post with "To the person in the red car" that way all the people in red cars that were driving in the town/village that morning will see your post and immediately enrol onto an advanced driving course.

- ❖ You've done your hair and makeup. You look amazing. You are so impressed you take a selfie and the world deserves to see it. Obviously, there are rules here. People can't know that you are feeling pretty good about the way you look today so my advice is to pretend the post is about something else. Ask a question. I find asking whether people think you should get your hair cut does the trick as that will invite people to tell you what you already know, your hair is amazing. Don't forget to filter it, people can't know what you actually look like.

- ❖ A little bit later in the year, or the following week, don't forget to throw back. Repost the fabulous photo (on throwback Thursday obviously) and make a statement to accompany it, maybe something like, "I can't believe I was thinking about cutting my hair".

❖ It's your child's birthday. Don't let the day go by without reminding people that your child is the funniest and most caring person ever to have walked the planet. Remind them to keep on being them. Your one year old child will be ecstatic when they read it.

❖ You've just cooked dinner, it looks great. Let everyone else know, share a photo, don't let this opportunity pass you by, people need to admire your chicken enveloped in a rich orange crumb accompanied by a chipped solanum tuberosum resting on a bed of curly kale. (Chicken nuggets and chips.)

❖ You've had an unfortunate accident, whilst you are bleeding profusely in the waiting room of A&E make sure you check in at the hospital. Then put your phone down, there is no need to respond to the 20 comments asking if you are ok, you don't want to worry anyone. If you require a drip of any kind remember to post a picture of your hand with the cannula in. #nofilter If you aren't lucky enough to have this particular prop, your wrist wearing a hospital tag will do.

- ❖ You haven't been out in a while, let everyone know that tonight, you are going out out.

- ❖ You have seen an accident on the road, you have no idea what has happened, but you wouldn't mind knowing the exact details as to how such a horror could have occurred. Be mindful that you don't want to appear nosy or intrusive. Instead ask if anyone knows if the victims are ok as it has worried you all day.

- ❖ You've driven past a dead cat. You couldn't stop because your child was in the car; however, it is your duty to post the unfortunate demise sending lots of owners of dark coloured cats into a blind panic.

- ❖ Politics. You know how the country should be run and you should let everyone know. Your unbiased views gained from extensive research on social media and a quick flick through the Sunday tabloids places you in a powerful position and it is your duty to pick apart government policy and let them know what they are doing wrong. It's not rocket science.

- ❖ One of the sad realities of social media is that not everyone is as clever and worldly wise as you. They will create posts that are wrong. You must let them know. Do not keep scrolling, they need to be educated. Put forth your argument (sorry, healthy debate) strongly and if appropriate back it up with links to dubious data sources that only agree with your point of view showing just how wrong they are. If, after 50 or so comments your point still hasn't been made, agree to disagree, you are the bigger person and you won't sink to this troll's level.

❖ You have secured a way to earn an extra income that involves selling massive cans of magic powder that when added to water will make sure the more body conscious among us lose weight instantly. Don't concern yourself with the fact that drinking only Nesquik every day for 12 weeks would probably achieve the same result. Yours is healthy and everyone needs to know. Your followers will enjoy seeing your travel cup of milkshake every morning for 12 weeks. They will be delighted with the before pictures of you standing in front of the mirror with barely a stitch of clothing on and they will be desperate to know how they too can lose weight and make money at the same time. If your photos don't appear to hit the mark, then start messaging people you haven't spoken to since playgroup. Don't be obvious. Start with general chit chat, comment on a few photos they have recently uploaded and then go in for the kill. It is not fair to keep this information to yourself, you want to share this wonderful opportunity. Don't mention that you would receive a signing bonus and you and your mentor will be getting 90% each of any sale. It is not a pyramid scheme.

- ❖ Whatever is going on in your life, there will be an inspirational quote to capture this moment. Trawl the depths of the internet and post that bad boy. Your followers will love it, they will relate to it, they will read between the lines and agree that yes, dancing in the rain is a true testament to how well you are embracing life, they aspire to be as strong as you are. Don't actually dance in the rain though, it's cold and will leave you feeling wet not empowered.

❖ Consider a daily countdown to your holiday, this will ensure the friendly neighbourhood burglar has plenty of time to prepare.

❖ Take policing into your own hands. Set up a crime watch group for your local community. Sit by the window and comment on any van that doesn't look as though it should be there. Run the number plates through that website you've heard about and comment that it doesn't have a valid MOT. If there are children at the park who are older than 3, direct a post at the parents, do they realise they are at the park? If a dog has done his business and it has not been removed, mention it, you may also want to include a friendly note that your doorbell camera has recorded the squat for prosperity and if it isn't removed you feel you have no other choice than to post the video.

* ❖ It's 5 o clock, or as you rather wittily put it, wine o clock. Advertise your functional alcoholic status by posting a picture of your favourite tipple. You deserve it, you've had a day. If it isn't 5 o clock, add to the humour by stating it must be 5 o clock somewhere.

* ❖ The humble brag. You are feeling rather pleased with your life, and you should let your followers know. Don't be obvious, here are some ways to let everyone know how perfect your life is without appearing smug. You've been promoted at work, it's so awkward having to manage your friends and tell them what to do now, you still feel like one of them, but you're not. People just don't seem to realise how difficult it is being a size 8. You are furious with the school for labelling your child

gifted. No child should be labelled. Your daughter got mistaken for your sister yesterday, it was just so embarrassing for her.

❖ You're in a new relationship. The world needs to know how happy you are. Check in at every location you and the love of your life visit, if you're not out, check in at home, the bolder among us may even go a step further and check in to bed. Post loved up selfies at every given opportunity, remembering the ironic hashtags, #posingagain #crazy Don't get too concerned that your like count dwindles with every photo, people are just jealous.

❖ Nothing beats a bit of ironic humour on a social media feed. You haven't had many likes on your posts about your angelic children in a while, you need to change up. Time to show the world you are a fantastic parent with a wicked sense of humour by posting pictures of your children crying and explaining the rather witty reason for this mini meltdown. You wouldn't let them draw on the wall, you wouldn't let them wear a bobble hat in summer, you wouldn't let them use the toaster as a bath toy, it really doesn't matter what it is just as long as a picture of your crying child gets the like count up.

- ❖ If you have found an item on the street or in the shop, hold it to ransom. Your post on social media should let everyone know that you are now the custodian of this item and that it is your responsibility to guard it with your life. You are not going to release it until you are provided with a full description of all matters related to the loss and a copy of a passport.

- ❖ You're a secret private detective. Your friend has mentioned that a person you went to school with hasn't been posting nauseating pictures of her and her husband for a few weeks. It is now your duty to find out why. After hours of extensive research into the "private life" of this person, scrolling through likes, mutual friends and the backgrounds of photos, you have deduced that the husband has run off with a suspected work colleague who happens to be the niece of the local butcher.

❖ You've had a stint in a reality TV show and now you are a celebrity/influencer. This means you can now make money by taking pictures of yourself in certain clothing ranges, doing makeup tutorials and going to particular restaurants. As long as you don't mind having a house full of things you would never have chosen yourself and going on holiday to places you never dreamed of, you are now able to navigate life without spending a penny (for six months until you cease to become relevant). The problem with this new-found fame is that no one wants to see a feed full of adverts. Get creative. I find the most popular way of advertising without advertising is to say that you've had loads of messages asking about the dress you wore last Friday (nobody asked) and then posting a link to the dress. Obviously, you need a little #ad so find the smallest font possible and hide this in the corner of the post. If you are asked to become a "brand ambassador" then you must reveal this to your followers as if you are announcing your run for Prime Minister. It is essential that you explain that you have been wearing their clothes/sitting on their sofas/admiring their makeup for years and this is a dream come true. Do not mention that you had been holding out for a Gucci collab but it doesn't appear that they want to be associated with a third rate reality show contestant who has a shorter shelf life

than a pint of milk.

How to sell
unwanted items

3

Time for a clear out? No more car boot sales, no more driving

onto a field at 6 in the morning being surrounded by vultures

before you've even parked, looking for silver and electrics. It's

never been easier to make money from unwanted

clothes/furniture. No more clogging up the garage with things

that you think you'll take to a car boot sale but never get around

to, just take a photo and upload it to an online marketplace, think

it's easy? Think again. Here is a list of things to consider before

dipping your toe into one of the most frustrating minefields of modern times, all to make £1 selling an emergency umbrella you bought when you got caught out in the middle of August.

- ❖ If you want £5 for an item, inflate the price. Whatever price you list an item for you will be haggled down. In fact, try putting an item on for 1p, I guarantee someone will ask if that's the lowest you will go. They might even offer you an alternative price, marginally lower than originally stated and if you stick to your guns and don't negotiate they will "just leave it then".

- ❖ It makes absolutely no difference if you state that it is collection only. You can bold that sentence, you can make it all capitals, you can mention it more than once, you will still get five messages in your inbox asking if you deliver. My advice here is to state that you will and then charge an exorbitant delivery fee.

- You are not a fitting room. However, you will be asked if they can come over and try something on. Personally, I can't imagine anything worse than standing on the doorstep watching a stranger adorn your clothing and um and ah over whether it is the right fit. It's a size 10, that's as far as a fitting goes.
- Don't get too excited by an "is this still available" message. You can respond instantly, and you will never hear from the person again. No reason, just gone, like the little patience you had left.
- If by some miracle you sell an item for the full asking price, expect immediate seller's remorse, you have obviously underpriced the item.
- Logistics. You have a wardrobe. You have scoured the internet for the original retailer, you have found the leaflet detailing all the dimensions and you have

uploaded this along with a photograph of the wardrobe. What you and the original retailer haven't considered is "Will it fit in a Ford Mondeo with the seat down?" Your opinion matters. You are expected to know the boot capacity of every car on the road and take a guess as to whether it is large enough to house large items of furniture that originally arrived in a lorry. If you don't know then guess, your skills in spacial awareness are second to none according to this complete stranger and they will take you at your word.

❖ So, you've spent the last hour quibbling over 50p, you've finally reached an agreement and organised a suitable collection time. Do not get your hopes up. The final part of this transaction is still up in the air. You sit waiting patiently… for nothing. I'm sure some people get a warped satisfaction imagining you sat on the edge of your seat waiting for the doorbell to ring. They won't show up and they won't offer an explanation, some are even bold enough to remove themselves from the buying chat, showing a complete lack of social etiquette and making you regret ever attempting to sell anything in the first place.

- ❖ If, by some miracle, the buyer does actually turn up at your door, expect one final insult. The buyer is over the moon. They have been invited to a last-minute fancy-dress party and this grey blazer is perfect. You now spend the rest of the evening wondering why all of your friends and family have failed to mention that you have spent the last six months walking around looking like Dr Evil from Austin Powers.

- ❖ The following morning expect a strongly worded email stating that your sizing is wrong. The blazer is not a size

10/12 as advertised (it is, it's written on the label). Apologise profusely and ask if they'd like their money back. Be informed it is not worth the extra fuel and the item is now in a charity bag. Spend the rest of the day fuming that you are somehow responsible for the fact that Dr Evil has clearly underestimated her dimensions.

❖ Sometimes, even offering an item for free will lead to no shows or more questions than a Mastermind final. It's considered bad form to shout but to be honest if you are getting something for free just come and pick it up, if you don't like it, sell it, at this point nobody cares.

How to participate
in a group chat

4

The group chat. One of the more useful tools in our arsenal. No more sending individual messages to friends organising a night out. Now you can all have the discussion together. Beware the pitfalls of a group chat though. Lurking behind this streamlined way of making our lives easier lies a million ways you can trip up, be cast out of your family or find yourself in a whole world of bother.

- ❖ You've been saying it for months but now the more decisive member of the group has decided you are all going to have a long overdue catch up. It seems straightforward, there's only four of you, how hard can this be? I think Houdini had an easier time trying to find his way out of a straight jacket. First, is it drinks, lunch, dinner or a coffee at home? This takes three days to decide. One is on a diet and isn't eating normal food. One is having renovations and can't possibly have anyone round. One is just establishing a routine with the toddler and doesn't want to disrupt it by either going out or having anyone over. One is taking part in dry January and doesn't want to be around temptation. You settle on dinner, the non-eating one will have soup but not bread and the teetotal will just have to exercise will power. With that decided, move on to location. Everyone offers up a venue, the fact that each one suggests the place closest to them is merely a coincidence. This will also take approximately three days. One is overpriced, one served a particularly questionable lasagne four years ago, one made the neighbour's cousin sit on the toilet for 48 hours and the other one has bad reviews on trip advisor. The new one that has opened up hasn't had an opportunity to offend anyone so you all settle on that. The decisive one of the group will ring and book. What day are we all available? This will take much longer than three days. Amidst Beavers, lack of child care, the Tuesday evening boot camp and a complete unwillingness to miss The Masked Singer final it is looking like you might all be available in six months time. When three people agree a date, it is customary for the fourth to suggest you go without them. This is not acceptable to the group and the debate continues. After much shuffling around you think you may have hit upon a date that fits everyone and you book. This is exciting, this is the furthest you have got with a night out in years. The week before sees a flurry of messages reassuring all that you cannot wait to catch up. Two days to go, what is everyone wearing. Jeans and a nice top, obviously. The day has arrived. One messages the group, they have a headache but they're sure they'll be fine. Around lunchtime a second messages the group, they've been summonsed to school to collect a child, it's coming out of both ends. Mid afternoon, a third chips in, they're having the worst day following a night of no sleep. By late afternoon the fourth calls it. Shall we rearrange. The vote gets seconded and it's decided they will reschedule. Everyone breathes a sigh of relief, that was close.

❖ The family group chat. There are several. Starting with the one every member of the family is in all the way down to the one with just the people you live with. The larger the group the more complicated it is. The problem is that it is very rare that every member of the family is actually participating in any given conversation so whilst two or three people are having a riveting conversation about what they watched on television the previous night, there are probably a further fifteen people that really could not care less. Leaving them with a dilemma. They can't remove themselves from the group because you are effectively removing yourself from your family. You can't mute the chat because you might miss something. Instead you just watch your phone lighting up like it's New Years Eve.

❖ Extracurricular activity group chat. You're a parent and your child has enrolled in the local sports team. There's a group for that. You get added to this group and now you get the same messages each week. Is training on? What time? Where is it this week? You then get the post match report each week, it's basically the same as the week before. This is followed by all parents and their thoughts on the latest match. Some of the members of the group chat have assigned themselves a name which makes no sense to the other members of the group. I'm sure their friends understand while they choose to go by the name Jesus wants me for a sunbeam, but it is lost on everyone else. If you're really lucky someone will send a message meant for another group. There's nothing quite like opening up your son's football chat to find a picture of a half naked parent trying to journal their Slimming World progress.

❖ The work group chat. Some employees like to add all to a group chat. This is not a good idea. Gone are the days that you could leave the office politics in the office. If the group is a sizeable one you can expect it to be pinging at all hours of the day. If there is a slight disagreement, people will take sides. This will lead to sub groups. The sub groups will then become awash with horror at what the other side have to say and become obsessed with picking apart every sentence. Members of the sub group will egg each other on to call out the person that dared to spark the debate in the first place. Mob mentality will take over. The phrase 'work place bullying' will be bandied about and the company will have no choice but to issue an email to let everyone know they are in no way affiliated with messaging groups outside the workplace.

❖ The leaving school parent group chat. The final day of primary school is approaching and some of the parents think it's a great idea to organise an event to celebrate this. Every parent in the class is added to the group chat and it quickly gets out of hand. Ideas are being thrown about as if it's a team meeting to organise Glastonbury. Children arriving in limos, commemorative hoodies, a fly past by the local aerobatics team, you name it, it's being bandied about as if this is an entirely normal way to transition from primary to secondary. Eventually the voice of reason steps in and suggests that all the children really want is a bit of fun with their friends and you can almost hear the collective sigh of relief from the more sensible parents that were sweating at the thought of spending £500 for their child to have an afternoon in the school playground. This then leads to an exercise in oneupmanship over who has the best contacts for hay bales and doughnut walls. My advice to anyone who is about to face this nightmare is to mute the chat.

Eventually, everyone will settle down and the children will be sat on the school playground with a cup of orange juice and a cocktail sausage and will be none the worse for not having the Red Arrows performing a display whilst Catherine Jenkins does a rousing rendition of We'll Meet Again. (Steven's Mum thought she knew a guy).

❖ When navigating all these different groups, it is vital that you keep your wits about you. Double check that you are sending the right message to the right chat. Whatever you do, you do not want to send a rather funny meme about a nun and a cucumber to your dear old grandmother who is still recovering from the time your cousin got the wrong group and sent an article about seven ways to enlarge your anatomy without surgery.

How to watch television

5

I realise that this is something we've all been doing all our lives and a list detailing how to do it seems rather redundant. I would have agreed with you about five years ago but now television viewing has become a science we could all do with taking a course on.

- ❖ With the invention of streaming, we now have a million options for our viewing pleasure. We can subscribe to a wide selection of streaming platforms and dip in and out of them at our will. Gone are the days that we watched whatever the BBC told us we were going to watch. We have choice. Far too much choice. So much choice in fact that you complain that there is nothing on.

❖ Sitting down to watch a film with your other half. Deciding on a film is not easy. There is always one of you that takes control of the remote and runs through the options. This is not their only job, they also have to keep an eye on the other one who is finding it difficult to stay on task and is far more interested in their phone, offering the occasional grumble at every suggestion because they've either seen it, or they can't stand that person ever since they appeared in a party-political broadcast canvassing for the wrong side. An hour later you are both still sitting there unable to make a decision, which is just as well as it is now 9 o clock and far too late to start a film.

- ❖ Every now and again a brilliant drama will get the country talking. It's everywhere, you cannot read the news, look through the socials or turn on the television without hearing about it. This is a disaster. Your preferred method of watching television shows is a good old binge. Which means that you have to wait at least six weeks to start the show and means that you now have to walk around with your eyes closed for fear of finding out a spoiler that will ruin the whole show for you. When you've finally watched it the rest of the country has moved on and you have no one to talk to about it.

- ❖ Likewise, baking competitions. Although you are perfectly happy to watch this week by week along with the rest of the nation, you have realised you are busy the night of the final. This is a disaster. You have two choices, either watch it as soon as you get home which could be past midnight, or you are going to have to go off grid for the next 24 hours to ensure that you do not find out who has won. Neither option is particularly appealing and leads to more stress than the baking finalists felt trying to make a to scale replica of the Taj Mahal out of brioche buns and lady fingers.

❖ You and your partner have started a new series. It's gripping. You haven't gone to bed on the same day you have woken up for the last few nights as you are completely hooked and one more episode takes precedence over sleep. Your other half has a night out planned this week and you already have withdrawal symptoms because you are not going to be able to watch the next episode. Or can you? Whilst you are sat at home alone you accidentally sit on the remote and you find yourself watching the next episode. This is incredibly bad form. People have divorced for less. You have cheated on your partner and no amount of apologies will make up for this heinous act.

❖ Some series offer the option to watch the whole series on their catch-up platform straightaway, this is like manna from heaven. Everyone else is watching it too. However, we are not all at the same bit. This leads to some very non-conversations about it. "Has anyone been watching blah blah blah?" Everyone gets animated, however, one has it on record and hasn't started it, another one is only halfway through the first episode and someone has watched the whole thing. No one can talk about it without giving anything away.

❖ Adverts. If you've ever watched television mid afternoon on a weekday then be prepared. You are now going to be planning your funeral, releasing equity in your house to give to your children and taking out a payday loan which you need to pay for the donkey you've ended up sponsoring because you were bored at 2:30 on a Tuesday afternoon. You've basically found yourself being part of a specialist group of people that either have the Grim Reaper circling whilst sharpening his scythe or are unemployed. You need to get a hobby, you don't need any more commemorative coins, stuffed donkeys or thank you pens from Michael Parkinson.

❖ On the subject of adverts, who is writing them? Whilst some chap is pottering in his garden a smartly dressed woman comes skipping in to tell the cheerful tale of the funeral she's just been to. It wasn't a somber affair because it was paid for in full before the death occurred and the deceased got to take advantage of a £50 Amazon voucher. If this isn't enough to warm the heart, then perhaps you might be better off thinking about the relatives that are about to find out that any inheritance they thought they might be receiving has now gone to support lions in Mozambique because the deceased found themselves watching television at 3:30 in the afternoon and it seemed like a good idea at the time.

❖ Although not as popular as they once were, the mainstream channels love a program that shows you where you are going wrong in life. From how to cook for your family, how to live minimally, how to lose weight or how to find your soulmate by taking all your clothes off and standing in a glass box. These 'experts' are on hand to patronise and shame the poor folk that really didn't know what they were signing up for, all in the name of entertainment. It leads us, the viewing public, to become experts as well and criticise and judge our way through the program. These people will then end the show transformed, they will never buy a frozen chip again.

- ❖ In days gone by, television provided a much-needed escape from reality. Especially the soaps, or as they are now called, long running dramas. Unfortunately, light entertainment cannot be found between 7:30 and 9:00 on a weekday evening. Instead the soap opera bosses have put themselves in direct competition with one another and the outcome is that we all now have to watch death, betrayal and substance abuse of an evening, each program trying to outdo the others with how sensitively and graphically they handle a gritty situation that the viewing public are probably trying to escape from. There's nothing quite like a teenage addiction to glue to put you off your evening apple.

How to be
a parent

6

Parenting is tough. Being responsible for tiny humans can be overwhelming and can have even the most well-rounded people sat in tears as these tiny dictators turn their once glossy world upside down.

- ❖ You've got the app, you've peed on a stick hoping for a smiley face, you've worked out your most fertile days, you're post coital pillow talk involves your legs high up in the air, so gravity can work its magic and thanks to the wonders of modern technology and a good helping of advice from the pregnancy forum, you are now with child. Find a quirky way to announce this momentous occasion, maybe order a t shirt with baby on board scrawled across the front. Wait for friends to respond to your announcement with "I'm so glad we can finally tell people" it's essential that people know they were important enough to be let in on the secret before everyone else.

❖ You are now the most important person in the world. You are growing life, and everyone should now have unfiltered access to the miracle that is occurring within. Discuss cravings at length, wait for other miracle growers to chip in with the cravings they had and take they're word for it that this means they know for certain the gender of your baby.

❖ You've paid to have a 3D scan and you can't believe the image staring back at you in all its sepia glory is going to be with you soon. You now have confirmation in a small envelope as to whether it is a boy or a girl and you can't wait to organise the party that will reveal this in spectacular fashion. Maybe popping balloons filled with pink or blue powder. Invite all your loved ones to the gender reveal and take centre stage as you self indulgently make a big show of revealing something you have no control over and pretending that whatever colour that pops out is the exact one you wanted, yes you already have 4 girls, but you would have been devastated not to have a fifth.

❖ Your baby has been born. You will now not sleep for the rest of your life.

- Over the next twelve months your baby will reach a million milestones. Luckily you received a pack of cards after the birth, more of an obligation than a gift, and you are now lumbered with the task of taking a photo of the baby propping a card up showing the world that s/he has had their first bowel movement.

- The early years will pass by in a flurry of dirty nappies and soft play. Soft play. The Devil's playground. They love it. This bacteria infested pit of balls and foam is Disneyland to any child under the age of 5. Some soft play centres try their best for the parents, they even include little coffee shops, so you can relax and enjoy some time with other parents whilst the children run themselves into a frenzy. Don't be fooled. You cannot sit in the coffee shop. You don't have time to enjoy a hot drink because you can't take your eyes off them for a second. By the time you've taken off your coat, your little darling will have shot off and be waving at you from the very top of the three-tiered scaffolding threatening to go down the zip wire, whilst Wayne, the 16 year old untrained fun coordinator looks completely out of his depth. By the time your two hours is up, you will leave this torture centre with your ears ringing vowing never to step foot inside this screaming hell hole again. Your child falls asleep as soon as you get home. You book for the following week.

❖ First day of school. The day is finally here, you are now free between the hours of 9 and 3. These will become the shortest 5 minutes of your life. You will drop them off in the morning and to be honest you may as well stay there because by the time you look at your watch again it will be time to pick them up. All the months of day dreaming about all the things you will get done during this time will become a distant memory as you realise you have entered an alternate dimension where time speeds up.

- ❖ First day of school obligatory photo. An essential part of the going to school process. Your child is wearing a pristine uniform that is far too big, a shirt and tie that will never be worn again as the polo shirt is much more comfortable and carrying a gigantic rucksack filled with nothing as everything is provided at school anyway. Stand your child by the front door and have them smile as though they are not on the precipice of the most terrifying moment of their life. Caption this moment with how grown up they are looking and mention you are crying.

- ❖ The time has come for you to give up what little control you had in the first place. You are now dictated to by the school and their rules. You no longer have the right to book a holiday or decide what your child can have for lunch. If you slip a rogue Penguin into their lunch box expect a strongly worded email on healthy choices. If you feel your family could benefit from a fortnight in Florida expect an e mail with the word UNAUTHORISED shouting at you making you feel like you've let them know you will be holidaying in Afghanistan.

❖ Mufti day. Expect three a week and be prepared to pay for the privilege of allowing your child to wear their own clothes (the ones you have already bought and paid for). Sometimes the school likes to buck the trend entirely and assign a colour, or worse, a pattern to your child's class. You must now find an item of clothing that is spotty. If you don't have any spotty clothing, panic. Get creative at ten o clock the night before and butcher a perfectly good t shirt with sharpies. Reassure your sobbing child that they look great and everyone else will be wearing the same thing. At the morning drop off watch as your child enters the playground surrounded by children with elaborate t shirts and jumpers that were definitely not knocked up the night before after a bottle of wine. Vow to read the emails sooner next time.

❖ Harvest festival. I don't think I really need to go into too much detail here, we've all been there. It's the night before, you've just found the letter about harvest festival at the bottom of the bag and you now have 12 hours to find a shoebox, decorate it to look 'autumnal' and fill it with things from your cupboard. Here's the dilemma, the contents of this shoe box are now a direct reflection on your household. You don't want to appear mean but neither do you want to sacrifice your overpriced bottle of elderflower cordial. A new letter this year has gone out asking if parents would like to nominate an individual to receive the shoe box. Nothing says 'your friend/relative thinks you're needy' more than a box full of baked beans and orange squash arriving on your doorstep.

❖ World Book Day. A wonderful day that celebrates the written word by encouraging children to dress up as their favourite book character. Your child does not want to be Harry Potter for the third year in a row which is a problem because that's the only book character you can think of. A quick google comes up with plenty of suggestions that your child will not entertain. Following a healthy debate, you have now agreed on a character and you have the evening to come up with an outfit with an assortment of boxes from the recycling bin, parcel tape and a bin bag. Don't forget to take a picture by the front

door to show everyone your creative skills. Vow to be
more prepared next year and order from Amazon.

❖ The Christmas play. One of the highlights of the school
year, your child is going to be a penguin and perform a
dance. If I'm being honest, I loved watching my children
in the Christmas play. MY children. Unfortunately, the
format nowadays appears to be that the classes take it in
turns to perform their part. Which means you have to sit
through every other class murdering Away in a Manger
and manhandling the Baby Jesus who quite frankly looks
like he wants to start turning water into wine much earlier
than the Bible states.

❖ Sickness. Schools are breeding grounds for little germs
which is unfortunate considering all teachers are
germaphobes. If your child dares to mention they feel a
little bit on the green side, you will receive a call

demanding their immediate exit from the school premises. On arrival you will find your child sat on the seat of shame with a bucket trying to hide the smile of someone who has been let out of prison early. You will be informed that your child is now not allowed to return for 48 hours. Expect a letter later on in the year expressing concern that your child's attendance has dropped two percentage points and they may be required to send you to prison.

❖ The latest craze. Every generation has them and this one is no exception. Expect your child to go mad for the latest tiny bit of plastic that serves no purpose whatsoever. Scour the internet and all the shops looking for this bit of plastic and come home empty handed to see the look on your child's face as you explain why you have let them down. When you do finally manage to secure the tiny bit of plastic and present it to your child like Simba from The Lion King the craze will have moved onto something else and here starts the problem all over again.

❖ On a similar note, the latest must have Christmas present. They have diligently written their list for Father Christmas, having gone through the modern-day equivalent of the Argos catalogue, the Amazon wish list. They have been polite and asked how the reindeer are getting on, then they've compiled the worst list of tat you have ever seen along with the much-coveted toy of the year. There is not a hope in hell that you are going to find this, but you will not be defeated. You will trawl the shops, you will spend hours and hours on the internet, you will join forums of five hundred other desperate parents on the same search. When all hope is gone you will find the item on eBay for a ridiculous price and try to justify spending an extra £500 on something that will sit in a box for the next ten years. After all of that work, all the effort, all the tears and the tiny little remortgage of the house, who gets all the credit? Father Christmas. The fictional character that has managed to convince children that if they don't get the present they asked for it is because they are on the naughty list, leading to years of therapy as they try to work out what they could have possibly done wrong, which will definitely cost more than the overpriced item on eBay.

❖ Internet crazes. Not to be confused with tiny plastic crazes. These internet crazes do not require money, they require a level of understanding so you don't march your child off to a doctor after a week of them flinging their arms up to their head or standing bobbing from side to side like a penguin. It becomes second nature to them; no longer can you stand in a queue without the small person standing beside you performing one of these peculiar routines. Don't be embarrassed though, there will be at least five other parents in the line trying to distance themselves from their own penguin.

- ❖ Food. On Friday they will love sausages. The following Friday they won't. That's it, no explanation.

- ❖ They are hungry at all times of the day except for meal times. Well, I say hungry, they're only hungry for certain things, fruit is not one of those things. They don't like it when your answer to their starvation is either to have a drink or suggest that they might be bored and for goodness sake don't show them a picture of what starving actually looks like, apparently that is quite traumatising.

- ❖ Bedtime. This is the time your child will all of a sudden remember everything they did today and feel the need to run you through it in minute detail. Listen. There will be a question and answer session after this diatribe and if you haven't kept up your child will start all over again. They will also realise they have become dehydrated despite you trying to get them to drink water all day. If, after you have tucked them in, you hear some banging from upstairs, don't worry, your child will have decided now is the perfect time to start tidying their room.

How to go
on holiday

7

We've all been deprived of sunnier weather in the last few years but now holidays are up and running. Read on for some helpful advice for going on holiday in the 20's.

❖ You've done your research, you've looked at the entry requirements for each destination and you are happy with your choice. You've priced up flights and hotels and you're about to reach the "book now" page. Hold on a minute, why has the price doubled? Because apparently if you feel you need more than one pair of knickers and a toothbrush for a fortnight on the beach you are going to have to pay to take suitcase. If you feel like you might want to sit next to the person you have chosen to go on holiday with then you are going to have to pay for the seats to be together. Unless you want to play roulette and run the risk of sitting in the middle of a stag party wearing t shirts with "what goes on tour stays on tour" emblazoned across the front. Apart from the stag who has "condemned man" written on his.

❖ The long-awaited day has arrived, and you are off. You deliberated not going to bed at all as your alarm is set for 2am however sense prevailed, and you are now on your way to the airport with a sense of excitement and heartburn. After circling the airport twice looking for the long stay car park and narrowly avoiding paying £5 for missing the turn and ending up in the drop off zone, you are now at the check in queue.

- ❖ You stand and wait patiently whilst a group of ten lads jump around with unbridled glee as they hand a bill board sized boarding pass to the guest of honour while the check in staff chuckle generously at this original idea as if it isn't the fifth time they've seen it this week.

- ❖ You've checked in and failed the "I won't set the beeps off" game at security. You collect your bucket of electronics and attempt to get dressed whilst stuffing everything into your bag at the same time, creating a bottle neck situation which sees you give up and walk off with only one shoe on and your trousers threatening to expose you as your belt trails behind you.

- ❖ Now it's time for the "now we're on holiday" moment. The pub. Yes, it's 4 in the morning, yes you have been struggling with heartburn and an unpleasant nauseated feeling since your alarm went off this morning, but it's absolutely socially acceptable to have an alcoholic beverage for breakfast, because you are on holiday. This moment will then be documented for all the social networks in the form of a boomerang picture cheersing with your travel companion, because it would be rude not to.

❖ You've made it on to the plane and all the years of wasted Game Boy time come into play. You now have to play Tetris with the overhead bins, mixed with a bit of street fighter gameplay with the person four rows up from you that now wants to use your storage because someone has already filled theirs with an oversized handbag and a giant hat. After admitting defeat and placing your hand luggage under the seat in front of you, you are now going to spend the rest of the flight with your knees around your ears as there is nowhere for your feet to go.

❖ You have an empty seat next to you. Could this be your lucky day? Absolutely not. Whilst you are planning what you will do with all this extra room a rather flustered looking passenger comes clinking up the aisle. They had got caught up in duty free and had to have their name called out over the tannoy. There are two types of seat neighbour on a plane, those that keep themselves to themselves, bother no one and enjoy their flight in peace, and those that don't. Clinks is the latter. They are going to spend the rest of the flight telling you about all the places you should visit when you arrive as this is the fifth time they have been, and they are on first name terms with all the locals.

- ❖ The flight takes off and now the mile-high car boot sale starts. Starting with refreshments and not stopping until you have spent an entire month's wages on some scented candles and a scratch card.

- ❖ You have reached your destination. As you stand on the steps of the plane the heat hits you like you've opened the dishwasher halfway through the cycle. Your holiday really does start here.

- ❖ If you have booked a package holiday, this is where the fun really starts. You are going to find yourself on a bus doing a tour of all the hotels in the area, dropping off one family at a time. You feel a sense of dread as you head towards a hotel that looks like something that wouldn't be out of place in a holidays from hell documentary. Names are called, and you are overcome with relief when your name doesn't come up and you watch on smugly as a man is getting daggers from the wife who is mumbling that this is the last time they put him in charge of organising the holiday. Conversely you approach a hotel that looks fantastic. Surely this is yours, surely your name is going to be called this time. Sadly not, this is just a here's what you could have won situation. Yours will be the last hotel following a two-hour rollercoaster of emotions. It sits rather averagely between Fawlty Towers and The Ritz. It could be worse.

❖ You've chosen to go all inclusive so on arrival you are presented with a plastic wrist band which must remain on your person at all times. This entitles you to all the watered-down plastic cupped drinks you could desire, plus unlimited access to the strangest combination of foods you could imagine. You will be having lamb curry and chips with a side of paella every night for fourteen days. Food poisoning is a risk, but you've paid for it so it's a risk you are willing to take. Breakfast will be food left over from last night repurposed to look brunchy. You've spotted a beach restaurant attached to the hotel, this will be extra.

❖ Your first morning and you are going to take advantage of the sunshine and have a day by the pool. Or that's what you thought. After your leisurely breakfast of lamb curry omelette, you head down to the sun loungers only to find they are all taken. No one is actually using them but they all have a towel or a flip flop on them. You rant for half an hour about how shocking this is, all the while planning to join in with this international sport first thing tomorrow morning. A quick note to mention that whilst it is common place to blame Germany for this particular problem, in my experience it is actually a British pastime and it's time we all owned up to it.

❖ You have managed to secure a couple of loungers and now you can while away your time with the book you've been saving and a little bit of pool dipping when it gets a bit too hot. Or so you thought. A shout goes up from a rather enthusiastic hotel rep… pool Zumba is about to commence. Off they go trying to get the hotel guests off their loungers, so they can all take part in the pool version of the cha cha slide. The best course of action in this situation is to pretend you are asleep. There is no way you are getting into the pool to spend half an hour waving your arms in the air whilst the 18 year old toned and tanned rep informs you that you are having fun.

❖ You have successfully avoided the fun and you are now free to relax. This is a perfect time to take a picture of the pool making sure your legs are in full view, knees in an upright position looking like a couple of well-done hot dogs.

- ❖ Your two weeks have flown by in a haze of day drinking by the pool and late afternoons in your towel, laying on the bed eating Lays crisps, which are actually Walkers, but they taste different on holiday. Your evenings have been spent with entertainment that wouldn't be out of place at the BGT auditions with the added anxiety of audience participation. You've taken part in a few games of bingo and won some free cocktails which are free anyway as you are all inclusive. Your well-deserved holiday has come to an end and it is time to go home.

- ❖ Back to reality, when anyone asks about your holiday mention that you didn't want to come home. Explain to them that although it is only a one-hour time difference you are finding it hard to beat the jet lag.

- ❖ A week after you have arrived home start reposting pictures of your hot dog legs with "take me back" written underneath.

- ❖ Start the countdown for next year.

How to navigate
your
20's and 30's

8

Not as straightforward as the title suggests. Navigating early adulthood is a tricky time, especially in this day and age where you can't pick up a magazine without seeing an airbrushed beauty with curves in all the right places thanks to a bit of photoshop magic, and wishing you looked like her. Here are some things to look out for...

❖ Extensions are no longer confined to the building work you have done in the vain hope of adding extra value to your house. Basically, if you can grow it, you can extend it. People watch on in surprise as the girl with the cute bob the night before is now sporting Rapunzel style hair. Eyelashes are being extended so much sunglasses are sitting a couple of inches off everyone's face and nails are so long it's a miracle anyone has the dexterity to do their jeans up.

- ❖ Eyebrows. A trend that is now making all women over 40 regret following the previous fashion must have. It was once the done thing to have tiny little barely there eyebrows, now it's all about how to get your eyebrows to take over your face. The bigger and darker the better. If you have overplucked, all is not lost, you can now have your eyebrows tattooed on. My advice to you if you do go down this route is to make sure you have no plans for the foreseeable. You are going to look like a couple of big slugs have made your face their home and there is no way you can present this to the world until the slugs have reduced themselves to well trained caterpillars.

- ❖ Botox. Once the signature look of the super rich woman in need of a little iron out around the eyes, Botox has now found its way into the daily lives of the 20 somethings who are unable to show an emotion as they are basically dead from the cheekbones up. No look of surprise or happiness from this generation, just impassive expressions for all occasions.

- ❖ Lips. Quite frankly, the bigger the better. It has become unacceptable to be happy with the lips you were born with. The pillowy lips trend has gone a step further and now it is not unusual to see 20 year olds walking around with hot dogs where their mouths should be looking like they had a run in with a bee hive.

- ❖ Active wear. Not just for the gym, this is now the uniform of choice and can be worn on all social occasions, from the school run to the weekly shop, the local bar to the city club. Unfortunately, the look only really works on those with a size 6 figure. Any attempt to pull off this comfortable level of sophistication if you are a size 10 or over results in comparisons being drawn between you and a marshmallow.

- ❖ Going out. Countless selfies must be taken at various points in the evening, these must be posted to social media. Hidden within these selfies must be the most boring post in the short history of social media. Boomeranged cheersing. Basically, a group of drinks going back and forth ad infinitum. It's uninteresting, it doesn't add enjoyment to any one's day and you might look completely mad trying to coordinate your drink in one hand whilst ensuring the perfect phone angle with your other hand, but it is essential to a night out in the 20s.

❖ Whilst out, make sure you look for a flower wall. This has been erected so that photo opportunities are not missed, and you can stand awkwardly wondering what to do with your hands as scores of people watch on waiting for their turn. Basically, the adult equivalent of standing by the front door in your uniform on the first day of school.

❖ Eating out. You are at a nice restaurant. Your food has arrived. Do not eat it. No food should be consumed at the temperature the chef intended. Instead wait for the food to go cold whilst you take hundreds of pictures of your plate to post on social media. The modern equivalent of saying grace before eating, for what we are about to receive, may our followers be truly grateful.

- ❖ The dating scene. It's tough out there. You've had a couple of unsuccessful relationships and a handful of first dates that didn't get past the plate photography. This is where the guard comes up. Everyone is alerted to the fact that you have your guard up. No one actually knows what this means, but it makes the person seem worldly wise with an important story to tell, even if it is just that the boy they fancied in primary school sent a love note to their friend and you're still not over the betrayal.

- ❖ Members of the local gym. On the off chance these 20 somethings are one of the minority that actually uses their gym membership for a body workout rather than a financial one, they must tell everyone. Social media is filled with pictures of changing room selfies and check ins.

❖ If a gym membership is not achievable then running is the next best thing, the runner must have their phone on them though. This run needs to be recorded, hopefully on a little app which will map the run and give the option to upload it to social media, detailing distance, speed etc. This is going into the boomerang category of most boring social media post ever.

How to navigate
a pandemic

9

Although I'm reluctant to write about the pandemic, it would be remiss of me not to include it in a book about navigating these modern times, especially since this has been the main topic of conversation since 2020.

❖ The new normal. A complete contradiction in terms, however this is how we justify the fact that things have changed in the last few years and a lot of people appear reluctant to go back to how they were. Whether it be businesses that have decided to save on heating large premises by making employees use their own heating and work from their bedroom, or the council who have decided to take a week off collecting the bins "due to covid".

- ❖ Masks. Over the last two years we have now become used to these annoying bits of elasticated cloth that we can't seem to find when we need one but the minute we stick our hands into our spring coat that was packed away last year we find three screwed up in a tiny ball along with some poo bags for the dog you bought during lockdown. It took some time to adapt to these masks, around every shop entrance you would find a dozen people patting their pockets down whilst gazing longingly at the pint of milk in the shop they are now not allowed to enter because their face is on display. As time went on it almost became second nature when leaving the house, wallet, phone, keys, mask. Now, we don't have to use a mask. Which now leads to everyone entering a shop feeling completely naked, there's something missing and you can't put your finger on what it is... until you spot the paranoid shopper wearing a Perspex mask who clearly did not get the memo that these things are next to useless. Still, if it makes that person feel safe, who are we to judge?

❖ Back in the old normal, scientists were bright intelligent people who had spent a lot of time and money on their education to become an expert in their field. Now, a qualification is not necessary. Social media, mainstream media and television shows are awash with people who have graduated from the university of life and know how to handle the pandemic. The agoraphobics among us will support a full lockdown for the next five years. The more sociable will be horrified that bars and restaurants have closed down and instead think that anyone who is vulnerable should live in a giant zorb for at least ten years and not ruin it for everyone else. Those that don't work in the travel industry support complete border shutdown and those that do work in the travel industry think that because our cases are so much higher than anywhere else in the world we should all be free to travel wherever we like.

❖ Key workers. One thing that is sure to divide a nation. Surely every job is essential. Apparently not. Now you can go on to a government list and find out just how valuable you are to the society. There's nothing quite like the feeling of complete redundancy when you realise that the job that is very much essential to your life is not deemed important enough to be considered key.

❖ Furlough. Another national divide. Why should I be working my fingers to the bone, putting in overtime and keeping the nation running when that person gets to sit at home and be paid for doing nothing. Why don't the people that are not on furlough realise that this isn't a choice and I would rather be working and have a bit of job security.

❖ Vaccines. We all rejoiced, they have developed a vaccine and now we can all be immune to this horrible disease that kills people but is "just a cold." Never in a million years did anyone anticipate the dawning of a new sport, two sides pitted against each other slinging mud, screaming bloody murder if you happen to find out the vaccination status of the person sitting next to you. On one side you have the vaccinated. They were called to action and they took their place in line to "do their bit". They wore their "I've been vaccinated" stickers with pride and rejoiced as they compared which vaccine they had with Joe down the road. People flocked to detail their side effects and talked at length about how they have read that their jab is better than the others, quoting phrases like mRNA technology as if they've just graduated with a first from Cambridge. Then you have the other side. They are anti-vax. They will not be Guinea pigs, they will not roll their sleeves up like sheep and they will send you articles to studies done where several participants suffered the indignity of having all limbs falling off and growing back in mysterious places. They know of several people who have not been the same since having the vaccine and they will not, under any circumstances participate in this little slice of state control. Until they realise that they will need to have this vial of poison if they ever want to enjoy an all-inclusive holiday to foreign climes again.

❖ The daily government briefing. The highlight of the furloughed persons day. It's five o clock and we will now be treated to an hour of graphs, statistics and previously unknown journalists trying to make a name for themselves by demanding apologies for events unrelated to the pandemic. Boris, the captain on the football pitch, with a couple of professors on each wing stands behind the latest three-part slogan shouting clearly and concisely the three rules to live by, until next week when it will change to a different shouty slogan that is either a bit more forceful, or some carefully worded piece of advice which gives hope to the nation that the pandemic is in retreat. It isn't. A short address on the days highlights and latest advice follows. The government apologises for the lack of PPE in the hospitals however they have designed a new badge that NHS workers can wear with as much pride as the four year old that won a participation medal in last years sports day. Onto the graphs. It makes grim reading and quite frankly puts you off your afternoon biscuit. Added excitement when a new graph is introduced although this excitement dwindles when you realise it is a collection of data showing how quiet the roads were at rush hour yesterday. This seems a little obvious considering the country is in the middle of a lockdown and anyone venturing further than their gate without a bag of shopping in their hand is likely to be fined. Now for the best bit. Questions from the media. Each week a new topic completely unrelated to covid comes to light that has got the nation talking and this will be dealt with by the journalists. Watch the professors become increasingly more uncomfortable as they are asked to weigh in on something that is not remotely sciencey. As the months go on we, the viewers, scream at the television that the journalists are on mute. We marvel at their inability to count as they ask four questions instead of the regulatory two. We wonder how the head of an internet forum on cross country running managed to secure a slot on this prime-time extravaganza.

❖ Then the daily briefings ended, leading to confusion, how do I know when day time ends, and the evening begins? How will we know if we need to be alert? Get used to it we do, which then means we go into a complete meltdown when it is announced that a briefing has been scheduled for this evening. What could this mean? We soon learn that we only need to panic when it is announced that Boris will address the nation in a pre recorded message. This is when you really need to prepare for Armageddon.

❖ Curtain twitching through lockdown. You've reorganised your cupboard, you've perfected sour dough bread and you've taken up playing the piano and have no trouble executing Tchaikovsky's Symphony No 5 in E minor. You're bored. The only thing left to do is stand by the window and observe. Giving your other half a running commentary on the activities just beyond your driveway. The couple at number 9 are on their third walk of the day. There's a car parked outside number 11, they must have a visitor. There goes Keith again, I don't know where he got his dinosaur outfit from, but doesn't it bring a smile to everyone's faces? Apart from Gladys at number 2 who pointed out it wasn't essential. Did you see John at number 14 today? He had his shopping delivered by Aldi, I bet he's livid he didn't secure his usual Waitrose slot. Did you see Pam at number 3 today going off to work, since when was she a key worker?

- ❖ Home schooling. Your home used to be your sanctuary from the hours of 9 -3. Now you are overrun with furloughed people, people who are working from home and worse than any of these, children that are now being homeschooled. If you had wanted to home school your children, you would have named them Rain and dressed them only in clothes that had been ethically sourced from an island in Fiji. Your children don't want to be taught anything by you, and quite frankly neither should they be. According to them the last time you did any maths was using an abacus during the plague of 1665. You wouldn't think that long multiplication could have changed that much but believe me, you're doing it wrong and it will be pointed out to you. I think any long-lasting effects on a generation of home schoolers won't be education based but more a psychological issue born from spending too much time with parents that don't understand how to do long division and accidentally walked in on the zoom show and tell in a dressing gown demanding they tidy their room. Did any learning take place in two years? It's doubtful. Unless of course you count memorising the government list of key workers in the vain attempt to shoe horn yourself into a position that might enable you send your child back to school where they belong.

❖ Working from home and zoom. What a wonderful world we live in. Now going to work means stumbling out of bed, grabbing a shirt and making sure your top half is presentable. As long as you log your computer on to whatever clunky platform your place of work deems passable then you are basically free to manage the day however you see fit. No more small talk with other employees you can't stand, no more keeping your head down when it's your turn to do the coffee run. You are your own person and you are going to be so productive. Just as soon as you finish this video on how to train a mongoose. The day is somewhat interrupted of course when it's time for the team meeting. Always a pleasure. Ten people log on to the meeting, all ten have now been in lockdown for a number of months and are relishing the opportunity to see and speak to someone new. All at the same time. Which means not a soul can be heard. The person heading the meeting is on mute and Janice in accounts is desperately trying to tell everyone about her neighbour that has a Thank you NHS sign in her front window but was seen having three walks on Tuesday with someone that did not look like her husband. The meeting is complete chaos as signs are held up telling Jeff he is on mute.

❖ The Thursday clap. Every Thursday at 8 o clock. A chance to see which neighbours don't appreciate free health care. It started off small, just a quick round of applause. It descended into a community display of one-upmanship. Banging hands together was not enough, it needed to be louder. The louder you are, the more you care. Someone comes out with a pan and a wooden spoon. The following week one pan turns into a whole set where lids are being smashed together with as much force as a 100mph road traffic collision. Keith sees his opportunity and does his rounds dressed as a dinosaur again, you know he is secretly thinking the cheering is for him as he does his lap like Usain Boltasaurus. The pots and pans become musical instruments, now we are all being treated to free concerts every Thursday as people drag out their grand pianos and start tickling the old ivories in a desperate attempt to go viral hopefully leading to a guest appearance on This Morning. Politicians and celebrities took to their own doorsteps to join in, nobody dared risk the wrath of the media if they publicly failed to show their support. I think it was some time in August that the worry began to set in. Generations to come will have children looking up mid clap asking their parents why they all gather on their doorsteps at 8 o clock to make a lot of noise. No one will know the answer, it was just something our parents did. The clapping came to an abrupt end.

❖ Bubbles. The introduction of bubbles was welcomed by single people that until this point had only themselves and the Tiger King for company. Now anyone that lived on their own could join another household in the form of a bubble. Bubbles began flying around all over the place. You couldn't move without hearing "it's alright, I'm in their bubble." Some people took this to extreme lengths and had more bubbles than a bath.

❖ Social distancing. It became unacceptable to be within 2 metres of another person that was not part of your bubble. If you were brave enough to venture to the shops, round stickers now littered the floor marking a safe distance. If you found yourself putting a toe out of place you would be publicly lambasted, either by the staff or a fellow shopper. Supermarkets became a one-way system where a forgotten onion in aisle two would just have to stay there unless you wanted to find yourself going around in circles for the best part of two hours.

❖ Panic buying. What a great insight into the human psyche. Toilet rolls became the latest must have item, posts were made on social media alerting the community that they've heard Aldi are having a delivery at midnight. Shelves became bare as people flocked to buy tinned soup. After a fortnight of panic buying a quick glance at the shelves showed that however bad things had become, people would rather die of starvation than stock the cupboards with oxtail soup.

❖ The pingdemic. We now have the technology to show if you've been within two metres of someone who then later tests positive. This app is now going to be the thing that saves us all. What no one had taken into consideration whilst dutifully downloading the app is that this piece of cutting-edge technology was going to grind the nation to a complete halt. Beryl, who hasn't been out in six months cannot understand how she has been pinged. Until she realises that her house is right by the path where people like to congregate after the school run to have a long chat about last nights covid briefing. Lorry drivers are pinging left right and centre and complete police departments are being run by one man nearing retirement who hasn't been pinged because he only has a Nokia 3320 in his glove box for emergencies. New guidance is issued by employers, turn the app off otherwise there won't be a business to come back to.

- ❖ Testing. Free home testing was available to all, now we didn't need to drag ourselves out to a drive through testing site manned by 16 people in high vis jackets standing around mouthing at you through your window.

Lateral flow tests became part of the every day routine of the more hypochondriacky among us. I'm not sure I could taste that biscuit, I'm sure my throat feels scratchy, I coughed once last night, I better do a test. People could be heard sneezing in Waitrose and then loudly explaining that it's alright, they've tested.

❖ A positive result. It's happened, it's finally got you, now you have the task of informing all and sundry that you have let the side down. You receive a phone call from a 16 year old in his bedroom who wants to know your exact movements in the last week and the contact details of all the people you have come into contact with. You now have a dilemma. You know your friend has rescheduled their 40th birthday party twice, it is now happening on Saturday and you have been in the company of ten of the attendees including the birthday girl. You may as well wear a sign that just has unclean written on it.

❖ You've done it, you've navigated the pandemic. Covid-19 is in retreat. Life is getting back to the new normal. What everyone had failed to predict is that part of this new normal is the introductions of variants. At first these new variants were named after the location of where they were first spotted, until the world realised that this was a surefire way to incite heinous xenophobia as people vowed never to visit India and Kent again. Now they are going through the Greek alphabet and we are learning to wrap our mouths around unfamiliar words, omicron, or omnicron as the less sophisticated among us like to call it. Where will it all end? Who knows. All I know is that in years to come we are going to look back at this time and laugh at the absurdity of an exercise allowance, a three pie limit at Tesco and a nation of people banging their hands together on a Thursday night to say thank you to an organisation that they now spend every waking hour telling anyone that will listen that it's not fit for purpose.

Mindless wonderings

10

Some things don't fit into a neat little chapter so here is a collection of things that crop up when going about your daily business.

❖ Single shoes on the dual carriageway. How did they get there? Why is there only one? Is someone waking up this morning wondering why there is only one shoe at the front door?

❖ Spontaneous human combustion. This is not as a big a problem as I thought it would be when reaching adulthood. As a child I always thought it was, although unfortunate, quite common place to erupt into flames for no reason whatsoever. However, you don't really hear about it anymore. Unless of course someone has attended an 80's party in a shell suit, then the whole place is talking about it, steering you away from the smoker's corner in case you suddenly go up in flames.

- ❖ Wire coat hangers. Where do they come from? My wardrobe is full of them and I have no idea why. I'm not a frequent user of the dry cleaners where these things are common place, so why do I have 50 struggling under the weight of a jacket? Households only actually need one and it isn't to hang clothes up with, it is to be unravelled and used as a drain unblocker.

- ❖ What is the appropriate thing to do whilst a room full of people sing happy birthday to you? Do you join in? Do you start waving your hands around like a conductor for the philharmonic? I actually think the best course of action is to look surprised, embarrassed and delighted all at once whilst attempting a small shoulder dance to let your serenaders know that you are really enjoying these 20 seconds of undivided attention celebrating your launch, an event that wasn't actually your achievement in the first place.

❖ Why have all the songs not been written yet? There are 12 notes. 12. Surely at some point we are going to start repeating songs, how long can this carry on for?

❖ Why do we spend so much time telling children not to talk to strangers and then on Hallowe'en we send them to strangers' doors to take sweets that we don't know the origin of and at Christmas we thrust them on to the laps of an old chap with a beard?

- ❖ If you've had to ask someone to repeat themselves three times, nod and laugh. It's irritating for everyone at this point and the ordeal needs to come to an end.

- ❖ If you've got no signal, hold your phone over your head, it won't help but it is standard practice to let everyone in the room know you are trying your best.

- ❖ Why is it so difficult to correct someone when they have called you by the wrong name? There doesn't seem to be a way to do it without appearing incredibly rude, which is ironic considering this person hasn't bothered to remember your name. If you don't correct them immediately you are going to have to be known by this new name forever, any other solution is just awkward.

- ❖ If the person at the front of the queue is having a loud argument with the shop assistant, look around at your fellow queuers and pull a face at each other that leaves them in no doubt that you do not support this public display. Do not make eye contact with the antagonist, they will try to recruit you as back up.

- ❖ There appears to be a fraction of people that would like to appear more intelligent than their brain actually allows. We all know at least one, if you don't it's quite probable that you are that one. Easy to spot. If someone changes their mind about something they've done a 360. They will formulate emails or social media posts referring to themselves as "myself". They will take part in social media quizzes that show their followers that their IQ is greater than Einsteins completely ignoring the fact they have just given their data to a highly suspicious company rendering the high IQ somewhat questionable.

- ❖ I have some serious concerns about missing people. Police regularly put out alerts about people who have gone walkabout, a photo generally accompanies this alert. The problem here is that the most recent photo of said person is not an accurate representation of what they actually look like. We now have a community searching for a person with a flower crown and retro sunglasses, pouting like a duck. It is unlikely that going forward anyone will be found.

- ❖ Other people's dreams. They're boring. You were in your house, but it wasn't your house, your friend was there but it wasn't your friend.

- ❖ Is there anything more awkward than listening to someone tell you a story that you shouldn't already know. Your acting skills are now coming into play and you find yourself trying to think how you would normally react and then completely overdoing it.

- ❖ "Are you free next Thursday?" One of the worst sentences you can hear. How about you tell me what it is you want me to do and then I'll let you know if I'm free.

- ❖ Naming of parenting styles. Ah, he's a helicopter, she's a tiger, a lawnmower, an elephant, who is coming up with these? What is the word for a normal, mainstream parent who lets their child take part in a normal amount of activities and doesn't feel the need to stand over a homework session like a prison warden? Something steady and reliable that gets the job done safely. A Volvo parent.

- ❖ Why do drivers immediately panic when they see an ambulance blue lighting through traffic. All of a sudden, the Highway Code goes out of the window and drivers take leave of their senses as they start mounting the roundabout, swerving into the path of pedestrians who are very shortly going to need the services of the ambulance that has just gone screaming by.

❖ Lunch menus. Gone are the days you could go out for lunch and order a cheese sandwich or a ploughman's. Now you have to navigate a lunchtime menu that you don't understand. Deconstructed sandwiches that really only belong in Ikea and naked burgers which are just round slabs of meat with a bit of lettuce because bread has overtaken the Kray twins in crimes against humanity.

❖ On the subject of eating out, why is it no longer acceptable to eat your flat pack sandwich off a plate. Now food is served to us on giant shovels accompanied by chips served in flower pots. Bring back chicken in a basket, that's just the right amount of exotica I need for my dining experience.

- There appears to be a small amount of supermarket checkout workers that feel the need to narrate your shopping. Comments on your choice of evening meal and the smell of new bathroom cleaner are harmless enough but as you eyeball the nit shampoo and thrush cream slowly working their way to the front of the conveyor belt any insights on these particular items are most certainly not welcome.

- Can we all agree that in this day and age it is unacceptable to not pay at the pump? You are in a hurry, the person in front of you has just finished refuelling, they gently place the hose in its holster, then they look up. Yup, they are going in. The sense of injustice takes over. The pump next to you is moving swiftly but you are now boxed in whilst you wait for the person in front to have a browse of the plastic footballs and bags of damp

logs that they aren't going to buy.

Conclusion

11

From pandemics to the threat of World War 3 and the majority of national treasures from the 70s onwards under threat of cancellation at any given moment, navigating our way through the game of life has never been more confusing.

In writing this book, it is my hope that we can all take a step back from the grind of daily life and look for the small moments in each day that bring a little smile. Whether it be from a chance encounter in a supermarket, to witnessing a full-blown argument on social media. There is plenty to smile about out there. If you remove the filter.

Printed in Great Britain
by Amazon

16211977R00070